CAN CEREBRAS DETHRONE NVIDIA'S REIGN?

The AI Hardware Showdown

A Story of Innovation, Competition, and the Fight for the Next Big Leap in Artificial Intelligence

Alejandro S. Diego

Table of Contents

Introduction

Artificial intelligence has grown into one of the most transformative technologies of the modern era, reshaping industries, streamlining processes, and pushing the boundaries of what machines can do. At the heart of this revolution lies AI hardware, the foundation that makes it all possible. AI hardware plays a critical role in powering the immense computations required for training and running complex AI models. Without the specialized hardware that supports these operations, the advancements we see today in machine learning, natural language processing, and other AI applications would be unimaginable. The ability of AI systems to process vast amounts of data efficiently and in real time is heavily dependent on the underlying hardware, making it a key player in this technological evolution.

For years, Nvidia has reigned supreme in the AI hardware space. Originally known for its graphics processing units (GPUs) in gaming, Nvidia's GPUs have proven remarkably versatile for AI workloads. Their ability to perform parallel processing—handling multiple tasks simultaneously—made them a natural fit for AI training and inference. Nvidia's hardware has become a staple in data centers worldwide, driving everything from self-driving car technology to advanced medical diagnostics. As AI models have grown in complexity and size, Nvidia has managed to stay ahead of the curve, building a reputation for delivering powerful, reliable, and efficient hardware solutions. This dominance extends beyond just hardware; Nvidia has also developed a rich software ecosystem, making it easier for companies to build, train, and deploy AI models using its technology. This combination of powerful GPUs and a robust software stack has solidified Nvidia's position as the undisputed leader in AI hardware.

However, the landscape is starting to shift. Enter Cerebras, a bold new player that aims to disrupt Nvidia's long-standing dominance. Founded with a singular focus on AI, Cerebras has developed a groundbreaking piece of hardware specifically designed to optimize AI workloads: the Wafer Scale Engine (WSE). Unlike Nvidia's general-purpose GPUs, the WSE is purpose-built for AI, offering unparalleled speed and efficiency in processing vast amounts of data. This innovation has caught the attention of the industry and has raised an important question: could Cerebras be the company that finally challenges Nvidia's reign in AI hardware?

This book seeks to explore that very question. In the following pages, we will delve into the rapidly evolving world of AI hardware and examine the battle brewing between these two technological giants. Through a detailed analysis of both companies' innovations, strategies, and market positions, we will uncover whether Cerebras has the potential to dethrone Nvidia or if Nvidia will adapt and maintain its supremacy in the ever-competitive AI hardware landscape. As AI continues to push the boundaries of what's possible, the outcome of this rivalry could shape the future of the industry for years to come.

Chapter 1: Nvidia's Reign in AI Hardware

Nvidia's rise to prominence in the world of AI hardware began not as an intentional pursuit of artificial intelligence but as a solution for the gaming industry. Founded in 1993, Nvidia initially focused on developing advanced graphics processing units (GPUs) for video games, where high-performance rendering and image processing were essential. The company's breakthrough came with the development of the GeForce line of GPUs in 1999, which revolutionized 3D graphics and quickly positioned Nvidia as a leader in the gaming hardware space.

However, the leap from gaming to artificial intelligence was a turning point that would ultimately reshape the company's future. While GPUs were originally designed to handle graphic rendering, their architecture also proved uniquely suited for the parallel processing demands of machine learning tasks. As the need for AI capabilities grew, particularly in areas like deep learning, researchers realized that GPUs could be used to accelerate the computations required for AI training, far surpassing the efficiency of traditional CPUs (central processing units). Nvidia's GPUs, with their ability to process thousands of parallel operations simultaneously, became an ideal tool for AI developers looking to train neural networks faster and more efficiently.

The tipping point came in the early 2010s, as AI research began to accelerate. Deep learning, which relies on large datasets and complex neural networks, became a focal point for advancements in AI. Nvidia seized this opportunity by not only continuing to refine its hardware but also by investing heavily in software frameworks tailored for AI developers. The release of CUDA (Compute Unified Device Architecture), Nvidia's proprietary parallel computing platform, played a pivotal role in this transition. CUDA allowed developers to harness the full power of Nvidia GPUs for a wide range of applications beyond gaming, including scientific research, autonomous vehicles, and artificial intelligence. This software development, combined with the hardware advancements, enabled Nvidia to offer an integrated platform that became essential for AI research and development.

By the mid-2010s, Nvidia had firmly established itself as the go-to company for AI hardware. The explosion of interest in AI technologies, from autonomous driving to natural language processing, created a surge in demand for the company's products. Nvidia's GPUs became the backbone of AI development in major industries, including healthcare, finance, and robotics. Data centers worldwide began to adopt Nvidia hardware to meet the growing computational demands of AI applications, solidifying the company's dominance in the field.

Nvidia's ability to innovate and stay ahead of technological trends has allowed it to maintain its leadership in AI hardware. Its GPUs are now central to many of the world's most cutting-edge AI projects, from training autonomous vehicles to performing complex data analyses. The company's strategic focus on both hardware and software, along with its foresight to invest in AI when the technology was still in its infancy, has kept it at the forefront of AI innovation. This rise, driven by a combination of technical expertise, market awareness, and forward-thinking, is why Nvidia continues to dominate the AI hardware space today.

Nvidia's GPUs became the standard for AI tasks due to their unique ability to handle the intense computational demands of artificial intelligence, particularly in the areas of machine learning and deep learning. While CPUs have long been used for general-purpose computing, they struggle with the highly parallel tasks required for AI workloads. In contrast, GPUs are specifically designed for parallel processing, making them far more efficient at handling the vast number of calculations that AI algorithms require. This advantage made Nvidia's GPUs a natural fit for the growing AI landscape, as they could accelerate the training of neural networks by processing multiple computations simultaneously, which is essential for developing models that need to analyze massive datasets.

The versatility of Nvidia's GPUs also played a key role in their widespread adoption. Initially known for their use in the gaming industry, where they were optimized for rendering 3D graphics in real time, GPUs were later discovered to be perfectly suited for AI tasks as well. This dual-purpose capability allowed Nvidia to transition smoothly from gaming hardware to becoming the backbone of AI research and development. Nvidia's GPUs offered not only raw power but also the flexibility to be applied across a wide range of industries, from data centers and scientific research to autonomous vehicles and healthcare. As more companies and researchers recognized the benefits of using Nvidia's hardware for AI, its GPUs became the standard in the field.

One of the key reasons Nvidia has maintained its dominance in the AI hardware space is its robust and integrated software ecosystem, which has been specifically designed to support and enhance AI development. The centerpiece of this ecosystem is CUDA, a parallel computing platform and programming model that enables developers to fully utilize the power of Nvidia's GPUs. CUDA allows developers to write software that can perform highly complex computations efficiently, unlocking the full potential of Nvidia's hardware for AI applications. This platform has been instrumental in making Nvidia's GPUs more accessible to developers, allowing them to build, train, and deploy AI models faster and more effectively.

Beyond CUDA, Nvidia has developed a suite of software libraries and tools that further enhance the capabilities of its GPUs. These include cuDNN, which is optimized for deep learning tasks, and TensorRT, designed to accelerate AI inference.

Together, these tools help developers optimize their models for both training and real-time applications, offering a seamless pipeline from development to deployment. Nvidia's software ecosystem not only enhances performance but also simplifies the AI development process, allowing developers to focus on innovation rather than the intricacies of hardware optimization.

Moreover, Nvidia's software stack is tightly integrated with popular AI frameworks like TensorFlow and PyTorch, making it easier for developers to leverage its GPUs without needing to learn entirely new programming paradigms. This compatibility has made Nvidia's hardware an essential component of the AI development process across a wide range of applications. Whether it's training massive AI models in data centers or deploying AI-powered tools in real-time environments, Nvidia's powerful combination of hardware and software ensures its continued dominance in the AI space.

The ability to provide an end-to-end solution for AI development—from the hardware that powers complex computations to the software that simplifies and enhances the process—has made Nvidia's GPUs indispensable. This integration of hardware and software has fostered a loyal developer community, further entrenching Nvidia as the standard for AI tasks across industries. By continually innovating both its hardware and its software, Nvidia has built an ecosystem that is not only powerful but also essential for companies and researchers looking to push the boundaries of artificial intelligence.

Nvidia's influence extends far beyond its origins in gaming, touching a wide array of industries that rely on advanced artificial intelligence and computational power. Through its GPUs and accompanying software, Nvidia has become a key player in sectors such as healthcare, autonomous driving, and gaming, providing the hardware backbone that powers cutting-edge technologies.

Each of these industries demonstrates how Nvidia's technology has shaped modern advancements, creating new possibilities and driving innovation.

In the gaming industry, Nvidia has long been a dominant force, revolutionizing the way games are developed and experienced. Nvidia's GPUs are renowned for their ability to render high-quality graphics in real-time, enabling immersive experiences for gamers across the world. Technologies such as Nvidia's Ray Tracing, powered by its RTX GPUs, have taken gaming graphics to new heights by simulating the behavior of light with unprecedented realism. This has allowed game developers to create more visually stunning and lifelike environments, enhancing the player experience. But Nvidia's influence doesn't stop with the gaming visuals. The company's AI technologies have also become increasingly integrated into gaming. For instance, Nvidia's DLSS (Deep Learning Super Sampling) uses AI to improve game performance by rendering images at lower resolutions and then upscaling them to higher resolutions, ensuring smooth gameplay while maintaining visual fidelity. This blend of AI and gaming showcases Nvidia's role in pushing the boundaries of what's possible in the gaming world.

In healthcare, Nvidia's influence is equally transformative. The immense processing power of Nvidia's GPUs has become crucial in advancing medical research, diagnostics, and patient care. One of the key areas where Nvidia's technology is making a significant impact is in medical imaging. Using AI, Nvidia-powered systems are helping to analyze complex medical scans, such as MRIs and CT scans, faster and with greater accuracy than traditional methods. AI models trained on vast datasets of medical images can detect anomalies, such as tumors or fractures, earlier and with more precision, enabling healthcare professionals to make better-informed decisions. Nvidia's Clara platform, designed specifically for AI-powered healthcare solutions, integrates AI models and medical imaging to streamline diagnostics and improve patient outcomes. In addition, Nvidia's GPUs are being used in drug discovery, accelerating the process of analyzing molecular structures and potential compounds, which traditionally would take years of research. This capability has proven especially crucial during times of crisis, such as the COVID-19 pandemic, where Nvidia's hardware was utilized to power simulations that helped researchers better understand the virus and work toward developing vaccines.

In the autonomous driving sector, Nvidia's impact is profound. As the push for self-driving vehicles intensifies, Nvidia's GPUs have become a critical component of the hardware used to train and operate autonomous driving systems. Nvidia's DRIVE platform provides the computational power needed to process the enormous amounts of data generated by sensors, cameras, and radar systems in real time, allowing autonomous vehicles to make split-second decisions on the road. The platform uses deep learning to interpret the environment, recognize objects, and predict the behavior of other vehicles and pedestrians. Companies like Tesla and Audi have integrated Nvidia's technology into their vehicles to enhance safety features and lay the groundwork for fully autonomous driving. Nvidia's work in this area doesn't stop with the hardware; the company has developed simulation tools that allow autonomous driving systems to be trained and tested in virtual environments, dramatically reducing the time and cost associated with real-world testing. This approach accelerates the development of autonomous vehicles while ensuring that safety standards are rigorously met.

In each of these industries, Nvidia's influence demonstrates how its GPUs have evolved from a focus on gaming to becoming an indispensable tool for AI and computationally intensive applications. From bringing hyper-realistic graphics to life in video games to aiding in the early detection of diseases in healthcare and making autonomous driving a reality, Nvidia's contributions continue to push technological boundaries. Its versatile hardware and AI-powered solutions have made it a leader across these diverse fields, setting the stage for further innovations that will shape the future of technology.

Chapter 2: The Cerebras Revolution

Cerebras emerged on the tech scene as a bold and ambitious startup with a singular mission: to revolutionize the field of AI hardware. Founded in 2016, Cerebras recognized early on that the traditional computing approaches used for artificial intelligence were reaching their limits. While companies like Nvidia had dominated the AI hardware landscape with their versatile GPUs, these chips were originally designed for general-purpose computing, adapted to handle AI tasks as they evolved. Cerebras took a different approach, deciding to focus on building hardware specifically optimized for the unique demands of AI workloads. Their goal was not to compete with existing technologies in the same way but to completely rethink how AI hardware could designed and implemented to unlock new levels of performance.

At the heart of Cerebras' vision is the idea that AI workloads are fundamentally different from other types of computations. AI tasks, especially those involving deep learning, require processing vast amounts of data quickly, often in parallel, which presents unique challenges in speed, memory access, and data movement. Traditional GPUs, although powerful, are limited in how much data they can process simultaneously due to their size and architecture. Recognizing these limitations, Cerebras set out to build hardware that would not only match the capabilities of GPUs but surpass them by focusing solely on AI-specific tasks.

The result of this ambition is the Wafer Scale Engine (WSE), the largest chip ever created for AI processing. Measuring 56 times the size of a typical GPU, the WSE represents a monumental leap in hardware design. By dramatically increasing the chip's size, Cerebras was able to pack more processing cores and memory directly onto the chip, bringing them closer to the data they need to access. This design allows the WSE to perform massive parallel processing, significantly reducing bottlenecks and increasing speed. The WSE can handle larger datasets with ease, making it particularly well-suited for the scale of modern AI models, which require enormous amounts of data to be processed simultaneously.

Cerebras' mission extends beyond simply creating faster or more efficient hardware. The company aims to fundamentally change how AI is developed and deployed by providing tools that enable researchers and enterprises to push the boundaries of what AI can achieve. By focusing on reducing the time and cost of AI model training and inference, Cerebras is opening up possibilities for real-time AI applications in industries like healthcare, finance, and autonomous driving, where speed and accuracy are critical.

As Cerebras continues to innovate, its mission is clear: to provide the AI industry with hardware that is not just incrementally better but exponentially more powerful than what has come before. By doing so, the company hopes to drive the next wave of breakthroughs in artificial intelligence, positioning itself as a serious challenger to established players like Nvidia.

The Wafer Scale Engine (WSE) is the cornerstone of Cerebras' ambition to revolutionize AI hardware, and it's considered groundbreaking for several key reasons. First and foremost, its sheer size sets it apart from anything previously developed in the field of AI processing. The WSE is the largest chip ever created, measuring over 56 times the size of a conventional graphics processing unit (GPU). This radical increase in size allows for more processing cores, more memory, and ultimately more computational power, making the WSE a unique tool tailored specifically for the intensive demands of artificial intelligence.

One of the most critical aspects of the WSE's innovation is how it addresses the inherent bottlenecks in AI computing. Traditional GPUs, like those developed by Nvidia, are general-purpose processors that have been adapted for AI tasks.

While powerful, these GPUs are limited by their size and architecture, which restricts how much data can be processed simultaneously. GPUs are designed to handle multiple computations at once, but they have to access data from outside memory banks, which slows down performance due to the constant movement of data between the processor and the memory. This inefficiency becomes particularly evident in large-scale AI tasks, where models often require vast amounts of data to be processed concurrently.

The WSE, by contrast, was designed from the ground up to eliminate these bottlenecks by focusing on AI-specific workloads. Its massive size enables it to house an unprecedented number of processing cores—hundreds of thousands more than a typical GPU. These cores are responsible for executing the parallel computations that are essential for AI tasks like training neural networks or processing large datasets. But the key advantage of the WSE lies in how it arranges its processing cores and memory. By placing the memory directly next to the cores, the WSE dramatically reduces the distance that data has to travel, speeding up processing times and reducing latency. This proximity between cores and memory is crucial in AI tasks, where the rapid exchange of data is a determining factor in performance.

Another revolutionary aspect of the WSE is its ability to handle large AI models in a single chip. In traditional systems, when a GPU reaches its capacity, tasks are often split across multiple chips, which leads to further delays as data is passed between them. This creates inefficiencies in both time and resource usage. The WSE, with its vast number of cores and enormous on-chip memory, can handle much larger models directly on the chip itself, without needing to split tasks across multiple processors. This makes it especially useful for training the most complex AI models, which are growing larger with each advancement in artificial intelligence.

The architectural differences between the WSE and Nvidia's GPUs are significant. Nvidia's GPUs, while optimized for parallel processing, are still constrained by their smaller size and traditional reliance on external memory systems. Their architecture is designed for versatility, allowing them to perform well across a variety of tasks, from gaming to scientific computing. However, this general-purpose design means that Nvidia's GPUs can't fully exploit the specific demands of AI workloads, particularly when it comes to large-scale data processing and model training. On the other hand, the WSE's design philosophy is entirely focused on AI, and it sacrifices general-purpose flexibility in favor of maximizing performance for deep learning and machine learning tasks.

In addition to its physical size and processing capabilities, the WSE also brings new levels of efficiency to AI computing. By reducing the number of times data has to move between external memory and the processing unit, the WSE consumes less power while delivering more computational output. This is a critical factor in AI development, as the growing complexity of models means that the energy costs of training AI are becoming a major concern. The WSE offers a solution by providing the raw computational power needed for modern AI tasks without the corresponding increase in energy consumption that comes with traditional multi-GPU setups.

Ultimately, the Wafer Scale Engine is groundbreaking because it changes the paradigm of how AI hardware is designed. Instead of incrementally improving existing technology, Cerebras has reimagined the chip architecture from the ground up to better meet the unique demands of AI. Its size, architecture, and efficiency make it a powerful alternative to traditional GPUs, offering a glimpse of what the future of AI hardware could look like when designed with AI at its core. This ability to process larger datasets faster and with greater efficiency sets the WSE apart and positions

Cerebras as a serious contender in the AI hardware market.

Cerebras' decision to focus exclusively on AI-specific processing represents a bold departure from the traditional approach to hardware development, which has largely centered on general-purpose computing. Most chips, including those designed by giants like Nvidia, are built to handle a wide range of tasks, from gaming and graphics rendering to scientific computing. While these general-purpose GPUs have proven highly adaptable, their flexibility comes at a cost. By trying to serve multiple computing needs, they often compromise on the efficiency and performance that could be achieved in more specialized tasks—especially in the rapidly advancing field of artificial intelligence.

Cerebras took a different path by recognizing that AI workloads are fundamentally different from the types of tasks traditional processors were originally designed to handle. Deep learning, the backbone of most modern AI applications, requires the processing of enormous datasets and the training of complex neural networks, tasks that are highly computationally intensive. These operations depend on the ability to perform massive parallel computations and move large amounts of data quickly and efficiently. General-purpose chips, no matter how powerful, are not optimized for these specific demands. Instead of tweaking existing technology to accommodate AI, Cerebras set out to design a chip from the ground up that was tailored to meet the unique needs of artificial intelligence.

This focus on AI-specific processing is evident in every aspect of Cerebras' hardware design, particularly in the Wafer Scale Engine (WSE). By building a processor that is far larger than any traditional chip and packing it with an enormous number of processing cores, Cerebras has created a tool that excels at the tasks AI developers need most: parallel data processing, rapid memory access, and the ability to handle extremely large models. Unlike general-purpose GPUs, which must balance multiple types of workloads, the WSE is laser-focused on AI tasks, allowing it to process data more efficiently and with greater speed.

One of the core challenges of AI is managing the data bottlenecks that occur when vast amounts of information have to be moved between the processor and memory. In traditional architectures, this constant back-and-forth slows down processing times and leads to inefficiencies. Cerebras has tackled this problem by integrating memory directly onto the chip, placing it closer to the processing cores. This design reduces the distance data must travel, cutting down on latency and allowing AI models to run faster. While general-purpose GPUs also aim to process data efficiently, their architecture is less optimized for AI's specific need for rapid and frequent data exchanges, which is why the WSE performs so well in this context.

Cerebras' focus on AI-specific tasks extends to its vision of how the future of computing should look. General-purpose chips are designed to handle a wide array of applications, which makes them versatile but also limits their potential for specialization. In contrast, Cerebras' philosophy is that AI is such a transformative and demanding field that it requires its own dedicated hardware. The idea is that by focusing entirely on the needs of AI—particularly tasks like training deep learning models, AI inference, and real-time data processing—they can push the boundaries of what's possible in ways that general-purpose chips cannot.

The WSE's architecture also reflects this AI-centric focus. Instead of designing a chip to handle a variety of operations at a moderate level of efficiency, Cerebras built a chip that is optimized solely for AI, with a massive number of cores to handle parallel processing and on-chip memory to minimize delays. The decision to prioritize AI workloads at the hardware level allows Cerebras to achieve performance metrics that general-purpose chips struggle to match, especially as AI models grow larger and more complex.

Moreover, Cerebras' strategy acknowledges that AI workloads are not just another type of computational task—they are becoming a dominant force driving the future of computing. With applications in industries ranging from healthcare and finance to autonomous driving and natural language processing, AI is evolving into a core component of technological innovation. By designing hardware specifically for AI, Cerebras is betting on the continued expansion of this field and positioning itself as a leader in AI development for years to come.

In contrast, companies like Nvidia have succeeded by leveraging their general-purpose GPUs to serve a variety of markets, including gaming, visualization, and AI. While these GPUs have been remarkably effective, particularly in AI training, they are limited by their need to accommodate other types of computing as well. Cerebras' singular focus on AI gives it the freedom to optimize every aspect of its hardware for this one purpose, leading to breakthroughs in performance and efficiency that would be difficult to achieve with a more general-purpose approach.

In summary, Cerebras' commitment to AI-specific processing rather than general-purpose computing is what sets it apart from competitors. By building hardware that is optimized for the unique demands of AI, the company has created a chip that is faster, more efficient, and more capable of handling the increasingly complex AI models of the future. This focus allows Cerebras to offer a solution that is not only different but, in many cases, better suited for the challenges of modern AI than the traditional GPU-based systems that have dominated the industry up until now.

Chapter 3: AI Inference – The New Battleground

AI inference is the process by which an already trained AI model is used to make predictions or decisions based on new data. While the training phase involves teaching the AI model by exposing it to vast amounts of labeled data, inference happens afterward, when the trained model is applied to real-world tasks such as recognizing objects in images, understanding speech, or predicting stock market trends. In essence, AI inference is the stage where the AI model demonstrates its learned capabilities, generating insights or actions from data it has never encountered before.

The importance of AI inference cannot be overstated, particularly in real-world applications that demand quick, accurate decisions. Whether it's a self-driving car navigating a busy intersection, a medical AI system analyzing scans for early signs of disease, or a virtual assistant like Siri or Alexa processing voice commands, AI inference is the mechanism that allows these technologies to function in real time. Inference must be fast and reliable, as delays or inaccuracies can lead to critical failures—imagine an autonomous vehicle not recognizing an obstacle in time or a misdiagnosis in a healthcare setting. The ability of an AI system to perform inference efficiently and at scale is essential to the success of many cutting-edge applications, and this is why hardware optimized for inference is so vital.

While AI training, which involves teaching models how to interpret data, dominated the early years of AI hardware development, the industry's focus has gradually shifted toward AI inference as more models are deployed in real-world applications. Training AI models is an incredibly resource-intensive process, requiring vast computational power and time to adjust the model's parameters until it can recognize patterns accurately. For years, hardware development was centered on making this training process faster and more efficient, with GPUs becoming the go-to tool for researchers and companies pushing the boundaries of AI.

However, once a model has been trained, the next challenge is deploying it in environments where it can generate predictions in real time. As AI technology matured and more models were put into practical use, the demand for faster, more efficient AI inference grew rapidly. Unlike training, which happens once over a long period, inference happens continuously—every time a model is asked to process new data. This continuous need for rapid responses places immense strain on traditional hardware architectures, especially as AI models become more complex and are tasked with making real-time decisions.

AI inference has now become a key focus for hardware development because it directly affects how AI can be used in everyday applications. Real-time inference is critical in sectors such as autonomous driving, where the AI system must analyze its environment and make immediate decisions to ensure safety. In finance, AI models are used to detect fraudulent transactions as they happen, requiring split-second processing to prevent losses. In healthcare, AI systems performing inference on patient scans need to provide quick, accurate results to assist doctors in making timely diagnoses. The faster and more efficient the inference, the more value AI delivers in these high-stakes settings.

Furthermore, as AI models grow larger and more powerful, the resources needed to run inference efficiently have skyrocketed. This has led to a surge in demand for hardware that can not only handle these advanced models but also do so in a cost-effective manner. Running AI inference continuously at scale can be prohibitively expensive, especially in data centers where thousands of models are deployed across vast networks. Hardware optimized for inference can help reduce costs by making these models more efficient to run, using less energy while delivering faster results.

The shift in focus toward inference is also driven by the growing number of AI-powered consumer applications. Virtual assistants, recommendation systems, facial recognition, and augmented reality are all examples of technologies that rely heavily on real-time AI inference. These applications need hardware that can perform inference tasks quickly and with minimal lag, providing seamless experiences for users. For instance, when a user interacts with a voice assistant, they expect an immediate response—any significant delay could degrade the user experience and reduce the technology's usefulness.

AI inference has become a critical focal point in hardware development due to its essential role in real-world applications that demand fast, accurate, and scalable AI-powered decisions. As more AI models move from the research phase into practical use, the need for hardware capable of supporting these inference tasks has grown significantly. The success of AI in industries like autonomous driving, healthcare, and consumer technology hinges on the ability to perform inference at lightning speeds, making it a central concern for hardware developers aiming to power the next generation of AI-driven innovation.

When comparing Cerebras' AI inference tool to Nvidia's GPUs, the most striking differences lie in their speed and efficiency. Both companies have developed cutting-edge hardware, but their designs reflect distinct philosophies regarding AI processing. Nvidia's GPUs have long been the standard for AI tasks, excelling in both training and inference, due to their versatility and ability to handle parallel computations across various applications. However, Cerebras has entered the arena with a chip specifically tailored to AI, designed to outpace traditional GPUs in both speed and efficiency when it comes to AI inference.

In terms of speed, Cerebras' Wafer Scale Engine (WSE) offers a significant advantage. The company has reported that its AI inference tool processes up to 1,800 tokens per second for models like LLaMA-13B, compared to Nvidia's GPUs, which traditionally operate at lower speeds for similar tasks. This is largely due to Cerebras' architecture, which allows for more processing cores and reduces data transfer bottlenecks by bringing memory closer to the data being processed. In contrast, Nvidia's GPUs, while powerful, rely on external memory systems that require frequent data movement between the processing unit and memory, which can slow down performance during high-intensity inference tasks. By keeping everything on a single chip, Cerebras drastically cuts down on latency, allowing for faster inference times, which is crucial in real-time applications like autonomous driving or live translation.

Efficiency is another area where Cerebras has made significant strides. AI inference tasks, particularly in large models, can be extremely resource-intensive, consuming vast amounts of power. Nvidia's GPUs, while effective, often require considerable energy to maintain their high levels of performance, especially when handling complex AI models at scale. Cerebras, on the other hand, has optimized its WSE to not only run faster but also consume less power for equivalent workloads. By reducing the number of data movements between different components and enabling more parallel processing directly on the chip, Cerebras delivers a more power-efficient solution. For companies deploying AI at scale—such as those running data centers or powering large-scale AI-driven applications—this reduction in energy consumption translates into significant cost savings, making Cerebras an appealing alternative for enterprises focused on both speed and sustainability.

These differences in speed and efficiency have major implications for industries that rely on fast, real-time AI inference. One such industry is

autonomous driving, where AI systems must process enormous amounts of data in real time to ensure safe vehicle operation. An autonomous car, for instance, relies on AI inference to interpret its environment by analyzing data from sensors and cameras, recognizing obstacles, and making decisions in a matter of milliseconds. Cerebras' faster processing speeds would allow autonomous vehicles to react more quickly to their surroundings, improving safety and performance. Nvidia's GPUs have been the dominant hardware choice in this sector, powering companies like Tesla and Audi's self-driving technologies. However, the promise of Cerebras' WSE could push the industry toward even more advanced, real-time decision-making capabilities, reducing the risks associated with delayed responses.

Another key example is **live translation services**, where AI inference must process language in real time to translate spoken words from one language to another. For applications like

Google Translate or speech translation tools used in international conferences or customer service, the speed at which an AI model can infer meaning and translate it into another language is critical to user satisfaction. Any delay in the process can create confusion or disrupt communication. With Cerebras' AI inference tool, the processing time is significantly reduced, allowing for faster and more accurate translations in real-time scenarios. Nvidia's GPUs are currently the backbone of many of these services, but Cerebras' performance gains could further enhance the fluidity and immediacy of live translations, making them more effective and accessible across a wider range of applications.

Other industries that stand to benefit from faster AI inference include **healthcare** and **financial services**. In healthcare, AI-powered diagnostic tools rely on inference to analyze medical images such as MRIs and CT scans, providing doctors with critical information about a patient's condition in a timely manner. Faster AI inference could mean earlier detection of diseases and more precise diagnoses, improving patient outcomes. Nvidia's GPUs have already proven their value in this field, with applications like AI-driven radiology tools; however, Cerebras' ability to process larger datasets more quickly could further streamline the diagnostic process, offering even faster insights into a patient's health.

In the **financial sector**, AI models are used to detect fraud, manage risk, and predict market trends. These models need to process vast amounts of financial data in real time to make accurate predictions and detect anomalies as they happen. Delayed inference could lead to missed opportunities or unchecked fraud. Cerebras' enhanced speed and efficiency offer financial institutions the ability to perform these tasks more rapidly and at a lower cost, giving them a competitive edge in fast-paced markets.

Overall, the comparative analysis between Cerebras' AI inference tool and Nvidia's GPUs shows that

Cerebras offers clear advantages in both speed and efficiency, particularly for AI applications that require real-time decision-making. While Nvidia has established itself as the dominant force in AI hardware, the specialized design of Cerebras' WSE positions it as a formidable challenger, especially for industries where speed and cost efficiency are paramount. As AI models grow larger and more complex, the demand for faster, more efficient inference tools like those offered by Cerebras is likely to increase, potentially reshaping the landscape of AI hardware development.

Chapter 4: The Technical Showdown – Speed and Cost

When comparing the processing capabilities of Cerebras' Wafer Scale Engine (WSE) and Nvidia's GPUs, it becomes evident that both companies have taken distinct approaches to handling the increasingly demanding workloads of AI tasks. Cerebras has developed the WSE specifically for AI, with a focus on maximizing parallel processing, minimizing latency, and significantly improving efficiency for large-scale computations. Nvidia, on the other hand, has leveraged its legacy in general-purpose GPUs, which are highly versatile but less specialized for the massive, data-heavy tasks that AI requires at scale.

The Wafer Scale Engine is a groundbreaking achievement in chip design, measuring over 56 times the size of a typical Nvidia GPU. This massive size allows Cerebras to pack significantly more processing cores—over 850,000—into a single chip. In comparison, Nvidia's GPUs, even the high-end models like the A100, feature significantly fewer cores. While Nvidia's GPUs excel in parallel processing, the number of cores in a WSE allows for far more simultaneous tasks, which is especially useful in deep learning and neural network computations.

Nvidia's GPUs are built to handle a wide range of tasks, making them extremely versatile. However, this general-purpose design leads to trade-offs in efficiency when compared to Cerebras' WSE, which is built solely for AI workloads. Nvidia GPUs rely on external memory systems, meaning that data must frequently move between the processor and memory, creating bottlenecks. This data movement increases latency and reduces processing speeds for extremely large AI models, especially during inference, where real-time responses are crucial. The WSE, by contrast, has its memory integrated directly onto the chip, reducing the need for data to travel between different components. This architecture makes the WSE far more efficient in processing massive AI models without the same data movement delays that Nvidia's GPUs encounter.

One of the key metrics for comparing the performance of AI hardware is token processing speed, which measures how quickly a system can process individual units of data, or "tokens," in tasks such as natural language processing (NLP). In this respect, Cerebras has positioned itself as a leader. For example, Cerebras' WSE can process up to 1,800 tokens per second for models like LLaMA-13B, compared to Nvidia's GPUs, which typically operate at slower rates for similar tasks. This difference in token processing speed is crucial because it directly impacts the real-world performance of AI applications.

In tasks such as NLP, autonomous driving, or real-time translation, every fraction of a second matters. Faster token processing means AI systems can respond more quickly to inputs, making decisions faster and providing results in real time.

This speed is essential in industries where immediate, accurate responses are critical, such as healthcare, financial services, or autonomous driving. For instance, in a live translation tool, faster token processing means smoother, more accurate translations with less delay between spoken and translated words. In autonomous driving, it allows AI systems to process sensor data in real time, improving the vehicle's ability to navigate and avoid obstacles.

Nvidia's GPUs are still highly competitive, especially in environments where versatility is required. They perform well across a range of AI tasks, but when it comes to specific high-speed requirements for token processing in large-scale AI models, Cerebras' WSE has the edge. The ability to process more tokens per second makes the WSE better suited for inference tasks that need rapid, real-time responses, particularly in applications where time and accuracy are non-negotiable.

One of the most compelling aspects of Cerebras' WSE is its cost efficiency, particularly for enterprises that run large-scale AI models or have data centers with high operational demands. The WSE's architecture allows it to process large AI models on a single chip, reducing the need for multiple GPUs working in tandem. Nvidia's GPUs, by contrast, often require several units to handle the same workload, particularly for large, complex AI models. This means that enterprises using Nvidia GPUs may need to invest in additional hardware to achieve the same performance levels, leading to higher upfront costs.

Cerebras' single-chip solution provides an immediate reduction in hardware complexity, which translates into lower operational costs. Having more processing power on one chip reduces not only the number of processors but also the energy required to move data between multiple chips. This energy-saving design has long-term financial benefits, especially for companies that rely on continuous AI inference, such as those running data-heavy applications in fields like autonomous driving or healthcare diagnostics.

Nvidia's GPUs, while versatile, tend to consume more energy when handling high-end AI tasks. For enterprises, this means higher electricity costs and the need for more robust cooling systems to maintain optimal performance, especially in large data centers. Nvidia's GPUs are known for being power-hungry when pushed to their limits in tasks like deep learning model training and AI inference. By comparison, Cerebras' WSE has been designed to minimize these operational costs by optimizing the energy use for its specific AI tasks.

However, cost efficiency for enterprises also includes more than just the energy and hardware expenses. There are additional factors such as ease of integration, developer expertise, and the cost of transitioning to a new platform. Nvidia, with its well-established software ecosystem and vast developer community, offers a level of integration and support that has been honed over years. For companies that have invested heavily in Nvidia's ecosystem, switching to Cerebras may require significant initial investment in retraining staff, rebuilding infrastructure, and reworking software to fit the new architecture.

Cerebras, while new, offers long-term savings through its efficient hardware and ability to handle massive workloads on a single chip, making it an appealing choice for companies looking to optimize for both performance and cost. Over time, enterprises that switch to Cerebras may recoup their initial costs by lowering their operational expenses and improving their AI processing speed and efficiency.

Cerebras' WSE offers a distinct advantage over Nvidia's GPUs in terms of processing power, speed, and cost efficiency, particularly for enterprises that are focused on AI-specific workloads. The WSE's architecture, with its massive core count and integrated memory, makes it faster and more efficient for token processing and real-time inference tasks. While Nvidia's GPUs remain versatile and powerful across a broad spectrum of applications, Cerebras' purpose-built design represents a major leap forward for companies that need to scale their AI capabilities without incurring the high operational costs associated with traditional multi-GPU setups. As AI models become larger and more complex, the demand for efficient, specialized hardware like the WSE will likely continue to grow.

The advancements in AI hardware, particularly with the introduction of specialized systems like Cerebras' Wafer Scale Engine (WSE), have far-reaching implications for AI developers and companies alike. These innovations represent more than just a step forward in processing power; they also open new doors for AI applications that were previously constrained by hardware limitations. AI developers, who have long had to work within the bounds of traditional GPUs, now have access to tools that can handle much larger models and datasets, reducing the time it takes to both train models and deploy them in real-world settings.

For AI developers, the ability to process more data simultaneously without the delays caused by data movement between external memory and processing cores is a game-changer. It means that models can be trained faster, allowing for quicker iteration cycles. This acceleration not only enhances productivity but also enables developers to explore more complex architectures and push the boundaries of what AI can achieve. In fields like natural language processing, image recognition, and autonomous systems, the ability to process data more efficiently can lead to breakthroughs in accuracy, speed, and overall performance. By minimizing bottlenecks, hardware like the WSE offers the possibility of developing AI systems that are not only more powerful but also more practical for real-time applications.

For companies, the introduction of this specialized hardware means that they can deploy AI models more effectively and at a lower operational cost. In industries like healthcare, autonomous driving, and finance, where AI is used to make real-time decisions, faster inference can lead to improved outcomes. In healthcare, for example, faster AI-powered diagnostic tools could enable doctors to catch diseases earlier, potentially saving lives. In autonomous driving, the ability to process sensor data more quickly could improve safety by allowing vehicles to react faster to their environment. In finance, faster fraud detection systems could prevent losses by identifying suspicious activities in real time. These improvements not only enhance the effectiveness of AI applications but also reduce the resources required to run them, making AI more accessible and scalable for businesses of all sizes.

However, despite these advancements, there are challenges when it comes to comparing benchmarks across different AI models. AI hardware, such as Nvidia's GPUs and Cerebras' WSE, are often optimized for different types of tasks, which can make direct comparisons difficult. Nvidia's GPUs, for instance, excel in versatility, being able to handle a wide range of applications from gaming to scientific computing, while Cerebras' WSE is specifically designed to maximize performance for AI tasks. Because of this, benchmarks that measure performance in one area, such as AI inference, might not capture the full capabilities of each system. For example, a benchmark that focuses on token processing speeds might show Cerebras' WSE as vastly superior, but it might not reflect the flexibility and ecosystem advantages that Nvidia's GPUs bring to the table.

Another challenge in comparing benchmarks comes from the diversity of AI models themselves. Different AI models have varying computational requirements, making it difficult to create a one-size-fits-all performance metric. A model focused on image recognition might require different hardware resources than a model designed for natural language processing. Therefore, a system that performs exceptionally well on one model might struggle with another. This variability makes it hard for companies to determine which hardware is best suited to their specific needs without testing multiple configurations in their own environments. For AI developers and businesses, this means that selecting the right hardware is not simply a matter of choosing the fastest or most powerful system, but rather understanding the specific demands of their AI models and finding the hardware that aligns most closely with their goals.

Moreover, the benchmarks that do exist are often based on specific tasks or models, which may not reflect the real-world performance of a system in diverse or unexpected scenarios. For instance, an AI model that performs well on standard benchmark datasets might encounter difficulties when applied to more complex, real-world data. This makes it challenging to evaluate hardware purely on benchmark scores, as they don't always account for the nuances of actual deployment environments. For companies, this adds another layer of complexity in choosing the right hardware for their AI infrastructure, as they must weigh not only the raw performance figures but also how those figures translate into their specific operational needs.

In conclusion, the advancements in AI hardware like Cerebras' WSE have profound implications for AI developers and companies. They open up new possibilities for faster model training and inference, reduce operational costs, and make AI more scalable and accessible. However, comparing these systems based solely on benchmarks can be misleading, as different models and applications place unique demands on the hardware. Ultimately, the choice of hardware should be guided by the specific needs of the AI models being used and the practical realities of their deployment, rather than relying solely on generalized performance metrics.

Chapter 5: The Hidden Costs of Switching

Moving from Nvidia's well-established ecosystem to Cerebras' Wafer Scale Engine (WSE) presents exciting opportunities for performance gains, but it also comes with a series of hidden costs that companies must carefully weigh before making the transition. While the speed and efficiency benefits of Cerebras' hardware are enticing, shifting from Nvidia to a completely different platform requires more than just the purchase of new equipment—it necessitates a broad reconsideration of how AI workflows are structured, how teams are trained, and how software is developed and integrated.

One of the most immediate hidden costs is the **hardware investment** itself. Nvidia's GPUs have been the standard for AI tasks for years, meaning that many companies already have large-scale infrastructures built around them. These infrastructures include not only the physical GPUs but also the surrounding systems designed to support them, such as data storage, cooling, and network infrastructure. Switching to Cerebras would require a significant upfront investment in new hardware, as the WSE is designed differently from traditional GPU-based systems. It's not just a matter of replacing GPUs with the WSE—companies would likely need to reconfigure their data centers to accommodate the different cooling requirements, power usage, and networking needs that Cerebras' technology demands. This represents a substantial cost, especially for enterprises that have already invested heavily in Nvidia's hardware.

Beyond the hardware itself, companies would also face costs related to **retraining staff**. Nvidia's ecosystem is not just about hardware; it includes a robust set of software tools, libraries, and development frameworks that developers and engineers have become deeply familiar with over time. CUDA, for example, Nvidia's proprietary parallel computing platform, is widely used by AI developers to optimize their code for Nvidia GPUs. Switching to Cerebras would require these teams to learn a completely new set of tools and paradigms. While Cerebras has developed its own software environment to work with the WSE, it is not yet as mature or widely adopted as Nvidia's, which means that staff would need time to adjust to the new system. Retraining costs can be significant, as it involves not only direct training expenses but also a potential slowdown in productivity as teams get up to speed with the new hardware. This learning curve can be particularly steep for enterprises that have built entire workflows around Nvidia's software stack, and the transition period could result in reduced output and efficiency until the teams are fully trained.

Another often-overlooked hidden cost comes from the need to **redevelop software infrastructure**. Nvidia's long-standing dominance in AI hardware has allowed it to build an ecosystem that integrates seamlessly with widely-used AI frameworks like

TensorFlow and PyTorch. Many companies have spent years developing custom software solutions that are deeply intertwined with Nvidia's GPUs, meaning that a switch to Cerebras could require significant rework to ensure compatibility. For example, AI models that have been optimized to run on Nvidia hardware using CUDA may need to be rewritten or adapted to work with Cerebras' system. While Cerebras does offer its own tools for model deployment and training, these tools are different from those used by Nvidia, and the transition may involve revising existing codebases, redesigning workflows, and redeveloping infrastructure to make the most of Cerebras' capabilities.

This redevelopment is not just a technical challenge but also a strategic one. Companies must assess whether the long-term benefits of switching to Cerebras, such as faster inference speeds and lower operational costs, outweigh the short-term disruption caused by restructuring their software infrastructure. For companies with deeply ingrained Nvidia-based systems, the cost of redevelopment can be substantial, as it involves not only adapting models but also rethinking the overall approach to AI development. This could mean hiring new staff with expertise in Cerebras' technology or investing heavily in consultation and support services to guide the transition. For businesses that rely on AI for critical, real-time applications, such as healthcare or autonomous driving, the risks of downtime or errors during this redevelopment phase can also be costly.

In addition to these tangible costs, there are **opportunity costs** associated with making the switch. During the transition period, teams may have less time to focus on innovation or improving existing models, as they will be preoccupied with adapting to the new hardware. This could slow down overall progress in AI development and make it harder for companies to stay competitive, especially in industries where time-to-market is crucial. Additionally, there is a risk that the early stages of adoption with Cerebras might not be as smooth as anticipated, particularly if the company is still refining its hardware and software offerings. Companies need to be prepared for potential setbacks or unforeseen challenges during the transition, which could add to the overall cost.

Ultimately, while the benefits of Cerebras' hardware, such as faster processing speeds and lower operational costs, are clear, the hidden costs of transitioning from Nvidia should not be underestimated. Companies need to consider the full scope of the investment, from reconfiguring data centers and retraining staff to redeveloping their software infrastructure. The decision to move from Nvidia to Cerebras is not just about upgrading hardware; it is a comprehensive change that affects every part of the AI development process, and the cost-benefit analysis must take these factors into account. For enterprises with established Nvidia-based systems, the transition may be complex and costly, requiring careful planning and a long-term perspective to ensure that the switch ultimately leads to greater efficiency and productivity in the years ahead.

Enterprises are often reluctant to shift from Nvidia to alternatives like Cerebras, largely because Nvidia has built an ecosystem that is not only powerful but also deeply integrated across various industries. Over the years, Nvidia has cultivated a level of trust through its proven track record of delivering high-performance hardware and a robust software ecosystem that developers know, understand, and rely on. This long-standing relationship with industries across AI, gaming, healthcare, and autonomous driving has established Nvidia as a de facto standard, making any shift to a different platform, like Cerebras, a significant and potentially risky undertaking for businesses.

One of the key reasons for this reluctance lies in Nvidia's **mature ecosystem**. Nvidia is more than just a hardware provider; it has developed an entire suite of software tools, libraries, and frameworks that simplify AI development and deployment. The CUDA platform, for instance, allows developers to take full advantage of Nvidia's GPU capabilities, offering optimizations that are difficult to replicate on other platforms. Many AI models are developed using CUDA, making them heavily reliant on Nvidia's hardware. Over time, companies have built their workflows, toolchains, and infrastructures around Nvidia's system, creating a tightly integrated setup that offers ease of use and familiarity for engineers and developers. Moving to Cerebras, or any new platform, would require breaking these existing systems and learning entirely new tools, which could be disruptive and costly in both time and resources.

The **trust** that Nvidia has built over decades also plays a crucial role in enterprise decision-making. Nvidia's hardware has been battle-tested across various industries, consistently delivering reliable, high-performance results in some of the most demanding environments. This reliability has created a sense of security for companies, particularly those working in fields where precision and accuracy are paramount. In industries like healthcare, where AI models are used to diagnose patients or suggest treatment options, or in autonomous driving, where real-time decision-making is critical to safety, any uncertainty about hardware reliability could have catastrophic consequences. The confidence that Nvidia's GPUs will perform as expected, based on years of proven results, is a powerful deterrent against switching to a newer, less tested platform.

Additionally, Nvidia's **extensive support network** and large developer community provide significant advantages. Because Nvidia's hardware and software are so widely used, there is a wealth of resources available, from developer forums to official support channels. This community-driven ecosystem allows developers to find solutions to common problems quickly and efficiently. For enterprises, this reduces the cost of maintaining AI systems and solving technical issues. In contrast, while Cerebras is making strides in building its own ecosystem, it lacks the same level of community support and depth of resources that Nvidia has cultivated over many years.

There are real-world examples of companies facing the difficult choice of whether to stick with Nvidia or explore alternatives like Cerebras. Take **Tesla**, for instance, which has used Nvidia's GPUs for training its autonomous driving models for years. Nvidia's technology has powered Tesla's AI capabilities, helping the company process data from its vast fleet of vehicles and continuously improve its self-driving algorithms. While Tesla has since moved to develop its own AI chips for inference in its vehicles, it continues to rely on Nvidia's hardware for large-scale training tasks. The decision to move away from Nvidia's ecosystem, even partially, involved significant investment in developing custom hardware and software to replace the capabilities Nvidia offered. It's a high-risk, high-reward strategy, but it underscores the complexity of transitioning away from a platform that has been integral to a company's operations.

Another example comes from the **healthcare industry**, where companies have been slower to adopt alternatives to Nvidia due to the high stakes involved in medical diagnostics and treatment planning. AI-driven imaging technologies, which are used to analyze scans like MRIs and CTs, depend on the reliable performance of GPUs to process data quickly and accurately. Nvidia's solutions, with their robust libraries and extensive support for deep learning frameworks, have become entrenched in the healthcare sector. Transitioning to a new platform such as Cerebras could offer faster processing for larger models, but it would also introduce new uncertainties in terms of hardware reliability and compatibility with existing AI models. For many healthcare providers, the potential for errors during the transition, coupled with the time needed to retrain staff and reconfigure software, makes sticking with Nvidia a more appealing option.

The **financial services industry** also provides an example of the complexities involved in making this switch. Large financial institutions use AI models to process transactions, detect fraud, and predict market trends in real time. Nvidia's GPUs have proven essential for these tasks, where speed and accuracy are critical. While companies might benefit from Cerebras' increased inference speeds, the cost and risk of transitioning an entire financial infrastructure away from Nvidia is a deterrent. Financial firms are particularly sensitive to downtime and errors, as these could result in financial losses or regulatory issues. Nvidia's long-standing reputation for reliability makes it the safer choice for many enterprises in this sector.

Ultimately, the **decision to switch** from Nvidia to Cerebras involves balancing the potential performance benefits with the risks and costs of moving to a new platform. Nvidia's mature ecosystem, reliable track record, and extensive developer support make it a tough competitor to beat. For enterprises that have invested heavily in Nvidia's technology, the hidden costs of transitioning—such as retraining staff, redeveloping software, and potential disruptions in AI performance—can outweigh the advantages of switching to a faster, more specialized hardware solution like Cerebras. The inertia created by Nvidia's deep market penetration and the trust it has built over years is difficult to overcome, especially for companies operating in industries where stability and predictability are more important than cutting-edge performance gains.

Chapter 6: Nvidia's Counterattack

In response to increasing competition and the rise of specialized AI hardware such as Cerebras' Wafer Scale Engine (WSE), Nvidia has made several significant developments aimed at defending its dominance in the AI hardware space. As the demands for faster, more efficient AI inference grow, Nvidia has sharpened its focus on optimizing its GPUs for AI-specific tasks, while also expanding its software ecosystem and enhancing developer support to maintain its market leadership.

One of Nvidia's key strategies has been the release of **new GPUs optimized for AI inference**. Recognizing the shift from AI training to inference, where models need to quickly generate predictions in real time, Nvidia has developed hardware specifically designed to handle these inference tasks more efficiently. The Nvidia A100 GPU, part of the Ampere architecture, is a prime example. Released in 2020, the A100 was designed with AI workloads in mind, offering up to 20 times the performance of its predecessors in AI inference tasks. It features multi-instance GPU (MIG) technology, which allows a single GPU to be partitioned into multiple smaller instances, each dedicated to different workloads. This flexibility makes the A100 ideal for data centers running multiple AI models simultaneously, ensuring that each model gets the exact amount of computational power it needs without wasting resources.

Nvidia's **Hopper architecture**, introduced with the H100 GPU in 2022, took these advancements even further. The H100 was specifically designed to enhance AI inference and model training, with a focus on large-scale language models and other high-demand applications. The H100 includes features like the Transformer Engine, which is optimized for the attention mechanisms used in natural language processing (NLP) models. This allows the GPU to process models such as GPT and BERT more efficiently, reducing both inference time and power consumption. Nvidia's ability to continually improve its hardware for AI inference demonstrates the company's commitment to staying ahead of the competition, particularly as more companies look for faster, more cost-effective ways to deploy their AI models.

In addition to new hardware, Nvidia has also strengthened its position by building an **enhanced software ecosystem** that makes it easier for developers to work with its hardware. Nvidia's CUDA platform, which allows developers to leverage the parallel computing power of GPUs, remains a central pillar of the company's strategy. Over the years, Nvidia has continuously improved CUDA, adding features and optimizations that help developers make the most of their GPU hardware. For example, CUDA now includes support for a broader range of AI frameworks, such as TensorFlow and PyTorch, allowing developers to seamlessly integrate Nvidia GPUs into their AI workflows. This deep integration ensures that companies using Nvidia hardware can continue to innovate without needing to overhaul their existing software infrastructure.

Moreover, Nvidia has expanded its range of **software libraries and tools** that are specifically tailored to AI tasks. TensorRT, a high-performance inference engine developed by Nvidia, helps optimize AI models for deployment on Nvidia GPUs. TensorRT allows developers to reduce the latency and memory footprint of their AI models, ensuring faster inference times without sacrificing accuracy. This is particularly important in real-time applications, such as autonomous vehicles and healthcare, where decisions must be made in milliseconds. By offering tools like TensorRT, Nvidia enables developers to maximize the efficiency of their AI models and get the most out of their hardware.

Another major component of Nvidia's software strategy is its **NVIDIA AI** platform, which brings together a suite of AI development tools, including pre-trained models, application frameworks, and optimized libraries. NVIDIA AI is designed to simplify the AI development process, making it easier for companies to train, test, and deploy AI models across different industries. It includes tools for AI-powered recommendation systems, conversational AI, and computer vision, all of which are optimized to run on Nvidia's GPUs. By offering these ready-to-use solutions, Nvidia lowers the barriers to entry for AI development, enabling companies to implement AI technologies without needing to build everything from scratch.

Nvidia has also focused on fostering a **thriving developer community** by providing extensive resources and support. The Nvidia Developer Program offers access to technical documentation, training materials, and forums where developers can share ideas and troubleshoot problems. Nvidia's commitment to supporting its developer community ensures that new and experienced developers alike can quickly get up to speed with its hardware and software, allowing them to create more powerful and efficient AI models. The company's frequent updates and improvements to its development platforms show a strong commitment to keeping its ecosystem relevant and valuable to developers across industries.

In recent years, Nvidia has also made strides in **cloud-based AI solutions**, recognizing the growing trend of enterprises moving their workloads to the cloud. The company's **NVIDIA GPU Cloud (NGC)** provides a cloud-based hub where developers can access pre-configured containers for AI training and inference tasks, all optimized for Nvidia hardware. This allows companies to scale their AI efforts without the need for significant on-premises infrastructure, providing greater flexibility and cost savings. The NGC platform supports a wide variety of AI applications, from training deep learning models to performing large-scale inference tasks, making it an attractive option for companies looking to accelerate their AI development.

By continually refining its hardware, expanding its software ecosystem, and supporting developers at every stage of AI development, Nvidia has positioned itself to maintain its dominance in the AI hardware market. While new competitors like Cerebras are pushing the boundaries of AI hardware with innovative designs like the Wafer Scale Engine, Nvidia's comprehensive approach—combining cutting-edge GPUs, optimized software, and strong developer support—ensures that it remains a formidable force in the industry. As the demand for AI inference continues to grow, Nvidia's ability to adapt and innovate will be key to defending its leadership in the field.

Nvidia's vast resources and ability to quickly adapt to market changes have been critical to its long-standing dominance in the AI hardware industry. Over the years, the company has demonstrated remarkable agility in responding to emerging trends, consistently staying ahead of competitors by leveraging its deep financial reserves, extensive research and development (R&D) capabilities, and strategic foresight. These resources give Nvidia a substantial advantage in a market that is constantly evolving, enabling the company to anticipate shifts and introduce innovations that meet the demands of both the AI and broader tech industries.

One of Nvidia's key strengths lies in its ability to allocate significant financial resources toward **research and development**. With billions of dollars invested annually in R&D, Nvidia can explore new technologies and rapidly develop products that push the boundaries of AI hardware. This consistent investment has allowed Nvidia to maintain its leadership in GPU development, particularly in AI training and inference. For example, when Nvidia recognized the growing importance of AI inference as more models moved from research into real-world deployment, it quickly pivoted to optimize its GPUs for inference tasks. This led to the development of the Ampere and Hopper architectures, which introduced features like multi-instance GPUs (MIG) and the Transformer Engine, specifically designed to improve performance for AI inference and natural language processing. These innovations showcase Nvidia's ability to identify emerging market needs and deliver solutions that address them effectively.

Another important aspect of Nvidia's adaptability is its **strong partnerships and strategic acquisitions**. Nvidia has consistently worked with leading companies in various sectors, from autonomous driving to healthcare, to ensure its hardware and software are widely adopted. Collaborations with companies like Tesla, Microsoft, and Amazon Web Services (AWS) have allowed Nvidia to integrate its technologies into large-scale applications, further cementing its influence across multiple industries. Additionally, Nvidia's acquisitions, such as Mellanox (for high-speed networking) and ARM (pending approval, aimed at enhancing its AI and mobile computing reach), reflect the company's forward-thinking approach. These acquisitions not only expand Nvidia's technological capabilities but also allow the company to enter new markets with minimal friction, staying relevant as industry needs evolve.

Nvidia's ability to **adapt quickly** is also seen in its response to the growing demand for cloud-based solutions. Recognizing the shift toward cloud computing and the increasing need for scalable, on-demand AI processing power, Nvidia developed its **NVIDIA GPU Cloud (NGC)** platform. This cloud-based solution allows companies to access pre-configured AI environments optimized for Nvidia's GPUs, enabling enterprises to scale their AI efforts without needing significant investments in physical hardware. By offering cloud solutions alongside its traditional on-premises hardware, Nvidia has ensured that its technology remains accessible to a wide range of users, from startups to large enterprises. This strategic move allows Nvidia to compete in the rapidly growing cloud AI market while maintaining its dominance in on-premises data centers.

Nvidia's **history of innovation** is another factor that sets it apart and helps the company remain competitive. Founded in 1993, Nvidia initially gained prominence in the gaming industry with its revolutionary graphics processing units (GPUs). Over time, Nvidia recognized that the architecture of its GPUs, designed for parallel processing, was ideally suited for handling the vast computational demands of AI, especially in deep learning. This realization led Nvidia to pivot from being primarily a gaming hardware company to becoming the leading provider of AI hardware solutions. The development of CUDA, its parallel computing platform, was a game-changer in this transition, providing developers with the tools needed to fully utilize the processing power of GPUs for AI tasks. CUDA's continued evolution has enabled Nvidia to remain a critical player in the AI ecosystem, with the platform becoming an industry standard for AI and machine learning development.

This **track record of foresight and innovation** is one of Nvidia's most significant assets as it navigates an increasingly competitive market. The company has consistently identified emerging trends—whether it be AI, autonomous driving, or cloud computing—and positioned itself as a leader in those fields. Nvidia's ability to develop not only cutting-edge hardware but also the accompanying software ecosystem ensures that it remains relevant and indispensable to developers and enterprises. For example, as AI models became more complex and required more specialized hardware, Nvidia developed the TensorRT inference engine and the DGX systems, tailored to accelerate deep learning tasks. By continually innovating both in hardware and software, Nvidia has maintained a competitive edge, offering end-to-end solutions that few companies can rival.

Nvidia's **response to competition** also highlights its ability to stay competitive in the face of emerging challengers. For instance, when companies like Cerebras introduced specialized AI hardware, such as the Wafer Scale Engine, Nvidia was quick to adapt by improving its own offerings for AI inference, training, and large-scale model processing. Rather than being reactive, Nvidia's strategy has often been proactive—anticipating trends and preparing its products to meet future demands. This adaptability ensures that Nvidia can defend its market share, even as new competitors push the boundaries of what AI hardware can achieve.

Looking forward, Nvidia's vast resources, history of innovation, and strategic adaptability position it well to face the future challenges of AI hardware development. As AI models become larger and more complex, requiring even more specialized hardware, Nvidia has shown that it has both the capability and the willingness to innovate at the cutting edge. Whether through developing new GPUs optimized for AI, expanding its software ecosystem, or making strategic acquisitions, Nvidia's ability to evolve with the market ensures that it will remain a dominant force in the AI hardware landscape for years to come. Its combination of financial strength, innovative culture, and strategic partnerships makes it uniquely capable of maintaining its leadership in an industry that is constantly changing.

Chapter 7: The Competitive Landscape

The AI hardware market is a rapidly evolving and competitive space that extends well beyond the major players like Nvidia and Cerebras. As the demand for high-performance AI computing continues to grow across industries, a wide range of companies—both large and small—are developing specialized hardware to meet the unique needs of AI tasks. From tech giants like Amazon Web Services (AWS), Microsoft, and Google offering cloud-based AI solutions, to smaller companies like Groq that are pushing the boundaries of niche AI hardware, the landscape is becoming increasingly diverse and dynamic.

Specialized cloud providers, particularly AWS, Microsoft, and Google, have emerged as key players in the AI hardware market, leveraging their massive cloud infrastructures to offer AI services at scale. These companies have built extensive cloud platforms designed to support AI workloads, providing businesses with the ability to access powerful AI hardware without the need for on-premises investments.

AWS, for example, offers **Amazon EC2 instances** powered by Nvidia GPUs, as well as its own custom-built AI chips, such as **AWS Inferentia** and **Trainium**. These specialized chips are designed to optimize AI inference and training tasks in the cloud, providing customers with highly efficient and scalable solutions. Inferentia is focused on AI inference, which allows businesses to deploy models faster and at a lower cost, while Trainium is designed for AI training, promising better performance and lower costs compared to traditional GPUs. AWS's integration of custom AI chips within its cloud ecosystem makes it one of the most powerful cloud-based AI platforms, giving enterprises the flexibility to choose the hardware that best suits their needs without having to invest in physical infrastructure.

Similarly, **Microsoft Azure** has positioned itself as a leader in AI through its **Azure AI** services.

Microsoft's cloud offering is powered by a mix of Nvidia GPUs and **Intel's Nervana processors**, and it provides extensive support for machine learning frameworks like TensorFlow, PyTorch, and Microsoft's own **ONNX**. Microsoft has also integrated **FPGAs (Field Programmable Gate Arrays)** into its cloud infrastructure, allowing customers to customize hardware acceleration for specific AI tasks. By offering a diverse range of AI hardware options in the cloud, Microsoft Azure appeals to enterprises looking to scale AI operations without the complexity of managing on-premises systems.

Google Cloud, too, has made significant strides in the AI hardware market through its **Tensor Processing Units (TPUs)**, custom-designed chips that are optimized for training and running large machine learning models. Google's TPUs are central to its AI services, offering high-performance computing capabilities for tasks like natural language processing, image recognition, and other deep learning applications. By integrating TPUs into its cloud platform, **Google Cloud AI** has become an attractive option for companies looking to harness the power of AI without building their own infrastructure. TPUs are especially valuable for users of Google's machine learning framework, TensorFlow, offering deep integration and performance optimization.

Beyond these cloud giants, a number of **smaller companies** are also making waves in the AI hardware market, offering highly specialized and innovative solutions. **Groq** is one such company, developing niche AI hardware specifically designed to tackle the intense computational requirements of modern AI workloads. Founded by former Google engineers, Groq has developed its own custom-built chips known as **Tensor Streaming Processors (TSPs)**, which are optimized for high-speed AI inference. Groq's hardware offers extremely low latency and high throughput, making it ideal for applications where real-time decision-making is critical, such as autonomous driving, financial trading, and healthcare diagnostics. The company's unique architecture allows for highly parallel processing, providing a new alternative to traditional GPUs for companies that need specialized solutions for their AI models.

Another notable player in the niche AI hardware space is **Graphcore**, a UK-based startup that has developed the **Intelligence Processing Unit (IPU)**, which is specifically designed for machine learning workloads. Graphcore's IPUs are built to handle the complex data flows and parallelism required by AI models, offering high performance and flexibility. Graphcore's hardware is used in a variety of applications, including natural language processing, computer vision, and reinforcement learning, providing an alternative to traditional GPU-based systems. With its innovative approach to AI hardware, Graphcore has attracted significant investment and is seen as a serious competitor in the AI chip market.

Other companies, such as **Mythic** and **SambaNova Systems**, are also exploring innovative AI hardware solutions. **Mythic** is focused on developing low-power, high-efficiency AI chips that are particularly well-suited for edge computing, where devices like smartphones, cameras, and IoT sensors require AI capabilities without access to large-scale data centers. **SambaNova Systems**, on the other hand, is creating hardware and software designed to simplify AI deployment for enterprises, with a focus on reducing the complexity and cost of running AI models.

These smaller companies are filling important gaps in the AI hardware market, offering **niche solutions** that address specific needs, such as reducing latency, improving energy efficiency, or optimizing for particular AI tasks. While they don't have the resources or market reach of Nvidia or the cloud giants, their innovations are helping to push the boundaries of what AI hardware can achieve, and they offer compelling alternatives for companies that have highly specialized requirements.

In summary, the AI hardware market has expanded well beyond the dominance of Nvidia and Cerebras. With the rise of cloud providers like AWS, Microsoft, and Google, companies can access high-performance AI hardware without the need for physical infrastructure, allowing them to scale their AI efforts more easily. At the same time, smaller companies like Groq, Graphcore, and Mythic are carving out their own niches, offering innovative and specialized hardware that addresses the specific challenges of modern AI workloads. This diversity in the market ensures that AI developers and enterprises have a wide range of hardware options to choose from, depending on their needs, goals, and budgets. As the demand for AI continues to grow, this competitive landscape will likely drive further innovation, providing even more advanced and tailored solutions in the years to come.

In navigating the increasingly crowded AI hardware landscape, both Cerebras and Nvidia have adopted distinct strategies to differentiate themselves and maintain their competitive edges. The two companies, while offering vastly different approaches to AI processing, are deeply aware of the growing competition from cloud providers, smaller hardware developers, and even in-house solutions developed by tech giants. As the market evolves, success will be determined by factors such as innovation, scalability, ecosystem strength, and the ability to address both current and future AI demands.

Cerebras has taken a bold approach by focusing exclusively on **AI-specific hardware**. Its Wafer Scale Engine (WSE), the largest chip ever made, is designed to handle the immense parallel processing required by deep learning models. Rather than competing with Nvidia's general-purpose GPUs, Cerebras has built its business around offering a **specialized solution** for the most demanding AI tasks, such as training enormous neural networks and running large-scale inference operations. By creating hardware that is purpose-built for AI, Cerebras aims to attract enterprises that require raw performance for cutting-edge AI research and deployment.

One of Cerebras' key strategies for navigating this crowded market is to capitalize on its **unique architecture**, which enables faster processing and lower latency for large AI models. Unlike Nvidia's GPUs, which rely on external memory systems, Cerebras' WSE integrates memory directly onto the chip, reducing data transfer bottlenecks. This architectural advantage allows Cerebras to differentiate itself as the go-to solution for organizations with massive computational needs. Moreover, by positioning itself as a **complementary technology** rather than a direct competitor to Nvidia, Cerebras has focused on solving the specific bottlenecks faced by researchers and enterprises that require extreme parallelism in AI tasks.

However, Cerebras faces challenges in **building out its ecosystem** to match Nvidia's vast developer and software support base. Nvidia has spent years creating an integrated suite of tools, libraries, and frameworks that support AI development, making it a trusted and reliable partner for businesses across a wide range of industries. To compete in the long term, Cerebras will need to continue expanding its software offerings and building partnerships that encourage widespread adoption of its hardware. While its technology is impressive, the long-term success of Cerebras may depend on its ability to **integrate seamlessly into existing AI workflows** and provide the same level of developer support that Nvidia has mastered.

Nvidia, on the other hand, has taken a more **holistic approach** to navigating the AI hardware landscape, leveraging its vast resources to maintain dominance while also expanding its portfolio to cater to specific AI needs. Nvidia's key advantage is its **mature ecosystem**, which includes not only industry-leading GPUs but also software platforms like CUDA, TensorRT, and a range of developer tools that are widely adopted in the AI community. This ecosystem has created a **strong network effect**—developers are already familiar with Nvidia's tools, and companies have invested in building their AI workflows around Nvidia's hardware.

To navigate this increasingly competitive market, Nvidia has focused on **continuous innovation**. The development of specialized GPUs optimized for AI inference, such as the A100 and H100, shows Nvidia's commitment to staying ahead of the curve by addressing the specific needs of AI tasks. Nvidia's ability to **adapt quickly** to market changes has allowed it to maintain leadership even as new competitors like Cerebras enter the scene. By offering both high-performance GPUs for training and specialized hardware for inference, Nvidia provides a **versatile solution** for businesses looking to implement AI at various scales, from research labs to enterprise data centers.

In addition to hardware, Nvidia's investment in **cloud-based solutions** has further solidified its position. By partnering with cloud providers like AWS, Google Cloud, and Microsoft Azure, Nvidia ensures that its GPUs are accessible to businesses that prefer not to maintain on-premises infrastructure. This move allows Nvidia to compete directly with the custom AI chips offered by these cloud providers, giving customers the flexibility to choose Nvidia-powered instances within a cloud environment. Nvidia's strategy of making its technology available both on-premises and in the cloud ensures that it remains relevant in an industry where cloud-based AI services are rapidly growing.

Factors Determining Long-Term Success

Several key factors will determine which companies, including Cerebras and Nvidia, succeed in the AI hardware space in the long term.

1. **Innovation and Technological Advancement**: AI hardware companies must continue pushing the boundaries of what is possible to stay competitive. As AI models become larger and more complex, hardware needs to evolve to support these new demands. Companies that can innovate rapidly, offering both performance gains and energy efficiency, will be better positioned to capture market share. Nvidia's long history of continuous innovation gives it an edge here, but Cerebras' unique architectural innovations provide it with a strong foothold, particularly for customers who need extreme parallelism and speed for their AI workloads.

2. **Scalability and Flexibility**: The ability to scale AI solutions across different

environments—on-premises, in the cloud, and at the edge—will be critical. Companies that can offer hardware solutions that work across a variety of settings, and that can scale to meet the needs of both small businesses and large enterprises, will have a significant advantage. Nvidia's partnerships with cloud providers and its investment in edge computing, combined with its versatile GPUs, make it a strong contender in this area. Cerebras, while focused on large-scale AI, will need to demonstrate that its hardware can be flexible enough to meet a range of enterprise needs beyond research labs.

3. **Ecosystem and Developer Support**: A strong ecosystem is essential for the widespread adoption of AI hardware. Nvidia's success has been built in large part on its ability to offer a complete solution—hardware, software, tools, and a supportive developer community. Companies that can foster similar ecosystems, making it easy for developers to integrate their hardware into existing workflows, will have a

better chance of long-term success. Cerebras will need to continue expanding its software and developer support to compete with Nvidia in this respect.

4. **Cost and Operational Efficiency**: Enterprises are always looking for cost-effective AI solutions, especially as AI models grow in size and complexity. Companies that can offer performance gains while reducing operational costs, such as power consumption and data center overhead, will have a strong competitive edge. Cerebras' WSE, with its reduced latency and energy efficiency for large models, offers compelling cost advantages in specific scenarios. Nvidia, however, benefits from economies of scale, making its hardware more affordable for a wide range of applications.

5. **Adoption Across Industries**: The ability to serve multiple industries—healthcare, finance, autonomous driving, and more—will be crucial for long-term success. Nvidia's established presence across these sectors gives it a head

start, but Cerebras' specialized hardware could carve out a niche in industries that need extreme AI processing power, such as scientific research and national security. The companies that can demonstrate real-world applications and solve critical problems across industries will be better positioned to grow their market share.

In conclusion, both Cerebras and Nvidia are navigating the crowded AI hardware landscape through distinct but complementary strategies. Nvidia's versatile approach, bolstered by its mature ecosystem and continuous innovation, gives it an edge in maintaining its dominance across a wide range of AI applications. Meanwhile, Cerebras is positioning itself as a specialized solution for companies needing the highest levels of computational power. Success in the long term will be determined by each company's ability to innovate, scale, support developers, control costs, and demonstrate value across multiple industries. The competitive dynamics of the AI hardware market will likely continue to push both companies toward even greater advancements, benefiting enterprises that rely on these technologies for the future of AI.

Chapter 8: The Future of AI Inference

Advanced AI inference, which refers to the real-time application of AI models to make predictions, recognize patterns, or make decisions, has the potential to reshape numerous industries. As AI hardware becomes more powerful and efficient, the ability to perform fast, accurate inference at scale opens up new possibilities for innovation. By accelerating the speed at which AI models can generate insights and decisions, advanced AI inference enables real-time analytics, enhances medical diagnostic tools, and drives the integration of AI into everyday consumer products, fundamentally transforming how these industries operate.

In the realm of **real-time AI-driven analytics**, businesses across industries stand to benefit from the ability to process vast amounts of data quickly and make instantaneous decisions. In sectors like finance, for example, advanced AI inference allows companies to monitor markets in real time, detecting trends or anomalies and making split-second trading decisions that could mean the difference between profit and loss. AI-powered algorithms can analyze millions of transactions and market signals in real time, offering financial institutions an edge in managing risk, optimizing portfolios, and detecting fraudulent activities before they escalate.

Retail is another industry where real-time AI analytics can offer transformative value. Companies can leverage AI inference to analyze consumer behavior in real time, optimizing pricing strategies, personalizing customer experiences, and managing supply chains more effectively. For instance, AI systems can analyze sales patterns and inventory data in real time, adjusting product recommendations or alerting retailers to potential shortages before they occur. By leveraging real-time data, retailers can better understand and respond to consumer needs, enhancing customer satisfaction and driving revenue.

The power of advanced AI inference is also particularly impactful in **medical diagnosis tools**, where the ability to process large datasets in real time can save lives. AI systems trained on vast amounts of medical data, including imaging, genomic sequences, and patient histories, can now deliver rapid diagnostic results, providing doctors with critical insights that can guide treatment decisions. For example, AI models applied to medical imaging can analyze MRI or CT scans in real time, detecting anomalies such as tumors, fractures, or other conditions with greater accuracy and speed than traditional methods.

In cancer treatment, early detection is often key to improving patient outcomes, and AI-powered diagnostic tools that leverage real-time inference can help identify subtle signs of disease that might be missed by human clinicians. By rapidly processing patient data, these systems can offer near-instantaneous diagnostic suggestions, helping doctors make more informed decisions and potentially saving patients from long diagnostic wait times. Moreover, real-time AI-driven diagnostics can assist in emergency situations, where quick and accurate assessments of patient conditions, such as strokes or heart attacks, are essential for timely interventions.

Another significant area of impact is **AI integration in consumer products**, where advanced AI inference brings intelligent features into everyday devices, making them more responsive, personalized, and intuitive. In **smart home devices**, for example, AI inference is used to enable voice-activated assistants like Amazon's Alexa or Google Assistant to process commands in real time, responding instantly to requests, such as controlling smart appliances, answering questions, or setting reminders. As AI hardware improves, these devices will become even faster and more capable, making them indispensable in households across the globe.

In the realm of **smartphones and wearable technology**, AI inference plays a crucial role in delivering seamless, real-time functionalities such as facial recognition, augmented reality, and health monitoring. Smartphones now come equipped with AI processors that enable real-time image processing for enhanced photography, enabling users to take higher-quality pictures and videos by adjusting exposure, focus, and color balance instantaneously. Wearable devices, such as smartwatches, rely on real-time AI inference to monitor vital signs, track fitness activities, and even detect health issues like irregular heartbeats. These real-time insights allow users to proactively manage their health and well-being, offering a personalized experience that is both convenient and empowering.

The automotive industry also benefits from AI inference in **autonomous vehicles** and **driver-assistance systems**. Real-time inference is essential for the safe operation of autonomous cars, which must process vast amounts of sensor data—including visual inputs from cameras, radar, and lidar—in real time to navigate the road, avoid obstacles, and make split-second decisions. AI inference allows these vehicles to understand their environment and react quickly to changing conditions, such as the appearance of pedestrians, other vehicles, or unexpected road hazards. As AI hardware becomes more advanced, we can expect to see more reliable and widespread use of autonomous driving technologies, potentially reducing traffic accidents and improving overall transportation efficiency.

Similarly, AI inference is integral to **driver-assistance systems** that provide features like lane-keeping assistance, adaptive cruise control, and automatic emergency braking. These systems use AI to analyze sensor data in real time and assist drivers in making safer driving decisions. As the underlying hardware continues to improve, these systems will become more advanced, offering even greater levels of safety and convenience for consumers.

In addition to these specific industries, **AI-powered consumer electronics** and **entertainment** are increasingly benefiting from advanced inference capabilities. In video streaming platforms, AI inference is used to make real-time recommendations, offering users personalized content based on their viewing habits. Gaming systems are also leveraging real-time AI inference to provide enhanced gameplay experiences, where the game world can respond dynamically to a player's actions. With the rise of virtual reality (VR) and augmented reality (AR), real-time AI inference allows for smoother, more immersive experiences that adapt in real time to user inputs and environmental changes.

The **energy sector** also stands to gain from AI inference, particularly in the management of smart grids and the optimization of energy consumption. AI systems can analyze real-time data from energy networks, identifying patterns and predicting demand to optimize energy distribution and reduce waste. By leveraging AI inference to manage power consumption more efficiently, energy providers can improve sustainability while reducing operational costs.

Advanced AI inference holds the potential to transform industries by enabling real-time decision-making, personalized experiences, and more efficient operations. Whether in the form of real-time analytics for businesses, life-saving medical diagnostics, or intelligent consumer devices, the ability to process data rapidly and accurately is becoming a critical advantage in the modern world. As AI hardware continues to evolve, driving down costs and improving performance, we can expect to see even more widespread adoption of real-time AI inference, further blurring the line between cutting-edge technology and everyday life.

Both Cerebras and Nvidia are playing pivotal roles in defining the future of AI technology, each taking distinct paths that are contributing to the rapid evolution of artificial intelligence. Cerebras has made a name for itself by focusing on highly specialized hardware designed specifically for AI workloads. Its Wafer Scale Engine (WSE), the largest chip ever built, breaks away from traditional hardware limitations by offering massive parallel processing power. This allows AI researchers and enterprises to train enormous models faster and run more complex inference tasks with greater efficiency. By addressing the specific needs of AI at scale, Cerebras has positioned itself as a solution for the most data-intensive tasks, enabling advancements in fields like scientific research, healthcare, and autonomous systems, where the ability to process vast amounts of data in real time can lead to groundbreaking discoveries and applications.

Nvidia, by contrast, has built its success on versatility and its ability to cater to a wide range of industries. Its GPUs, initially designed for graphics, have become the gold standard in AI processing due to their ability to handle the parallel computations required by machine learning and deep learning models. Nvidia has expanded its influence by continuously improving both its hardware and software ecosystems, ensuring that its products are not only powerful but also accessible to developers. With innovations like the A100 and H100 GPUs, optimized for AI inference and training, Nvidia continues to lead in delivering high-performance solutions for industries as diverse as autonomous driving, finance, healthcare, and gaming. Its commitment to building an ecosystem that includes developer tools, software libraries, and cloud integrations has made Nvidia indispensable to companies of all sizes, allowing them to scale their AI efforts seamlessly.

As AI models become larger and more complex, both Cerebras and Nvidia are shaping the future of AI by pushing the boundaries of what is possible. Cerebras is likely to drive innovation in areas that require extreme computational power, such as training the largest neural networks and running highly specialized tasks that demand unparalleled speed and efficiency. Nvidia, with its adaptable GPUs and strong developer support, will continue to dominate industries where flexibility and scalability are key. Both companies are enabling the development of next-generation AI models that require real-time processing of vast datasets, which will be essential for applications like autonomous vehicles, medical diagnostics, and personalized consumer experiences.

Looking ahead, the next big breakthrough in AI hardware could come from several different areas. One possibility is neuromorphic computing, a field that mimics the structure and functioning of the human brain. This technology has the potential to revolutionize AI by processing information more efficiently and with less energy than traditional architectures. Companies like Intel and IBM have already begun exploring this area, and as neuromorphic chips become more advanced, they could offer a completely new way to tackle AI workloads, especially in tasks like pattern recognition and decision-making, where human-like processing could yield significant improvements.

Quantum computing is another area where future breakthroughs could emerge. While still in its early stages, quantum computing promises to solve certain problems far faster than even the most powerful classical computers. For AI, this could mean exponential improvements in optimization, data simulation, and large-scale processing tasks. Companies like Google and IBM are leading the charge in quantum computing research, and while it may take years for practical applications to emerge, the potential for quantum AI is immense.

Closer on the horizon, the next leap in AI hardware might come from advances in energy-efficient designs, particularly for edge computing. As more devices, from smartphones to autonomous vehicles, require AI capabilities at the edge, there is a growing need for hardware that can perform inference locally without relying on cloud computing. This trend toward edge AI will drive the development of smaller, more power-efficient chips that can deliver real-time AI processing while consuming minimal energy. Companies like Nvidia and startups like Mythic and Graphcore are already exploring these possibilities, and further innovation in this space could bring AI capabilities to a wider range of devices and applications.

Energy efficiency in AI hardware is becoming increasingly important as AI models grow in size and complexity, demanding more computational power and higher energy consumption. Future breakthroughs could focus on reducing the power required to run large-scale AI models while maintaining or even increasing performance. Cerebras' WSE is a step in this direction, with its ability to process large datasets more efficiently than traditional GPU-based systems. As AI continues to expand into industries with sustainability concerns, the demand for greener, more efficient hardware will likely drive significant advancements.

Another area of potential breakthrough is in the development of custom AI hardware designed for specific tasks. As AI applications become more specialized, there will be a growing demand for hardware optimized for individual use cases, such as medical imaging, real-time language translation, or autonomous navigation. Companies that can create AI chips tailored to these specific industries will have a competitive advantage. Cerebras, with its focus on AI-specific processing, and Nvidia, with its wide array of flexible GPUs, are both well-positioned to lead this trend. By developing hardware that meets the unique needs of different sectors, these companies could drive the next wave of innovation in AI technology.

In summary, Cerebras and Nvidia are actively shaping the future of AI by advancing hardware that meets the growing demands of modern AI applications. While Cerebras focuses on highly specialized solutions for extreme computational tasks, Nvidia continues to dominate through its adaptable, ecosystem-driven approach. Looking ahead, the next big breakthroughs in AI hardware may come from neuromorphic and quantum computing, energy-efficient designs for edge AI, and custom hardware for specialized tasks. As these technologies mature, they will likely redefine the capabilities of AI and open up new possibilities for industries worldwide.

Conclusion

The competition between Cerebras and Nvidia has introduced exciting possibilities in the AI hardware space, with both companies carving out distinct positions in the market. Nvidia, with its long history of innovation, has remained a dominant force, thanks to its versatile GPUs, robust developer ecosystem, and ability to adapt to the rapidly changing landscape of AI. Its hardware powers a vast range of industries, from autonomous driving and healthcare to gaming and finance, and its continual advancements, particularly in AI inference and training, have ensured that it stays at the forefront of AI technology.

Cerebras, on the other hand, has chosen a different path by focusing on creating specialized AI hardware designed to push the limits of what is possible in deep learning and neural network processing. The Wafer Scale Engine (WSE) has positioned Cerebras as a leader in handling the most demanding AI workloads, offering massive parallel processing power and reducing data transfer bottlenecks, all while driving performance for large-scale AI models. Cerebras represents the cutting edge of AI-specific hardware, providing solutions for industries that need extreme computational capabilities, such as scientific research and national security.

Throughout this book, we have explored how these two companies are shaping the future of AI technology, each with its unique approach. Nvidia's adaptability and strong ecosystem have made it the go-to choice for businesses that need versatile, scalable AI solutions, while Cerebras is pioneering new frontiers in AI processing by addressing specific bottlenecks and offering unprecedented speed for specialized tasks. Both companies are driving the AI industry forward, helping to realize the potential of artificial intelligence in applications ranging from real-time analytics and medical diagnostics to consumer products and autonomous systems.

As for whether Cerebras has a realistic chance of dethroning Nvidia, the answer is complex. Nvidia's deep-rooted presence in the AI ecosystem, supported by its robust hardware, software, and developer community, gives it a significant advantage in terms of market dominance. It has established itself as an industry standard across multiple sectors, and its continued innovation in AI hardware ensures that it will remain a key player for years to come. However, Cerebras is uniquely positioned to challenge Nvidia in niche markets that require extreme computational power and speed. In these specialized fields, Cerebras' technology offers a level of performance that Nvidia's general-purpose GPUs cannot match.

The ongoing competition between these two companies is likely to spur even further innovation. As Nvidia continues to optimize its GPUs for AI tasks and expand its cloud and edge solutions, Cerebras will likely push forward with more breakthroughs in AI-specific hardware. This rivalry benefits the entire AI industry, as it drives the development of faster, more efficient, and more specialized hardware, allowing businesses and researchers to tackle problems that were previously out of reach. As AI technology continues to evolve, this competition will ensure that companies remain focused on delivering hardware that meets the ever-growing demands of AI applications.

For readers, the future of AI hardware is full of potential, and staying informed about developments in this space is crucial. The technologies that power AI are rapidly changing, and the impact of these advancements will be felt across industries worldwide. Whether it's through faster AI inference, more energy-efficient systems, or new breakthroughs in neuromorphic or quantum computing, the AI hardware landscape is set to transform how we live, work, and interact with technology. As Nvidia and Cerebras, along with other emerging players, continue to innovate, it will be fascinating to watch where the next big leap in AI hardware comes from.

In conclusion, while Nvidia's dominance is well-established, Cerebras' unique approach to AI-specific hardware makes it a formidable contender in certain areas. The ongoing competition between these two companies is set to fuel the next generation of AI advancements, and it's an exciting time to follow the developments in this field. To stay ahead, readers should continue to engage with the latest news and breakthroughs in AI hardware, as the future of artificial intelligence promises to be even more transformative than what we have seen so far.